BRITISH HISTORY

The Victorian Age

1837–1914

Kingfisher Publications Plc
New Penderel House, 283–288 High Holborn
London WC1V 7HZ
www.kingfisherpub.com

Material in this edition previously published by Kingfisher Publications Plc
in the *Children's Illustrated Encyclopedia of British History* in 1992

This revised, reformatted and updated edition published by
Kingfisher Publications Plc in 2007

3TR/0907/PROSP/(RNB)RNB/128MA F

4 6 8 10 9 7 5 3

A CIP catalogue record for this book is available from the British Library.

ISBN 978 0 7534 1480 4

Printed in China

Consultant: Valerie St Johnston
Editor: James Harrison,
with Jean Coppendale and Honor Head
Designer: Edward Kinsey
Proofreader: Sarah Hewetson
Indexer: Christine Bernstein
Cover design: Mike Davis

CONTENTS

THE VICTORIAN AGE

(1837 – 1913)

THE PERIOD FROM THE ACCESSION of Queen Victoria to the outbreak of World War I has been called the Age of Empire. The British empire reached its greatest extent, covering one fifth of the world's land area, and containing one quarter of the world's population. During this period there were two reigns and the beginning of a third: Queen Victoria (1837 to 1901) was the last of the Hanoverian line which had started with George I. After her came Edward VII of Saxe-Coburg (1901 to 1910); this period is called the Edwardian era. George V was the last of the Saxe-Coburgs and the first of the House of Windsor.

The Victorian age witnessed great progress in medicine and public health, which helped to improve the lives of working people in the industrial cities. Social evils such as child labour in mines and factories were also abolished. More adults had the right to vote, though women were still excluded. The coming of the railways heralded a new age of travel for everyone.

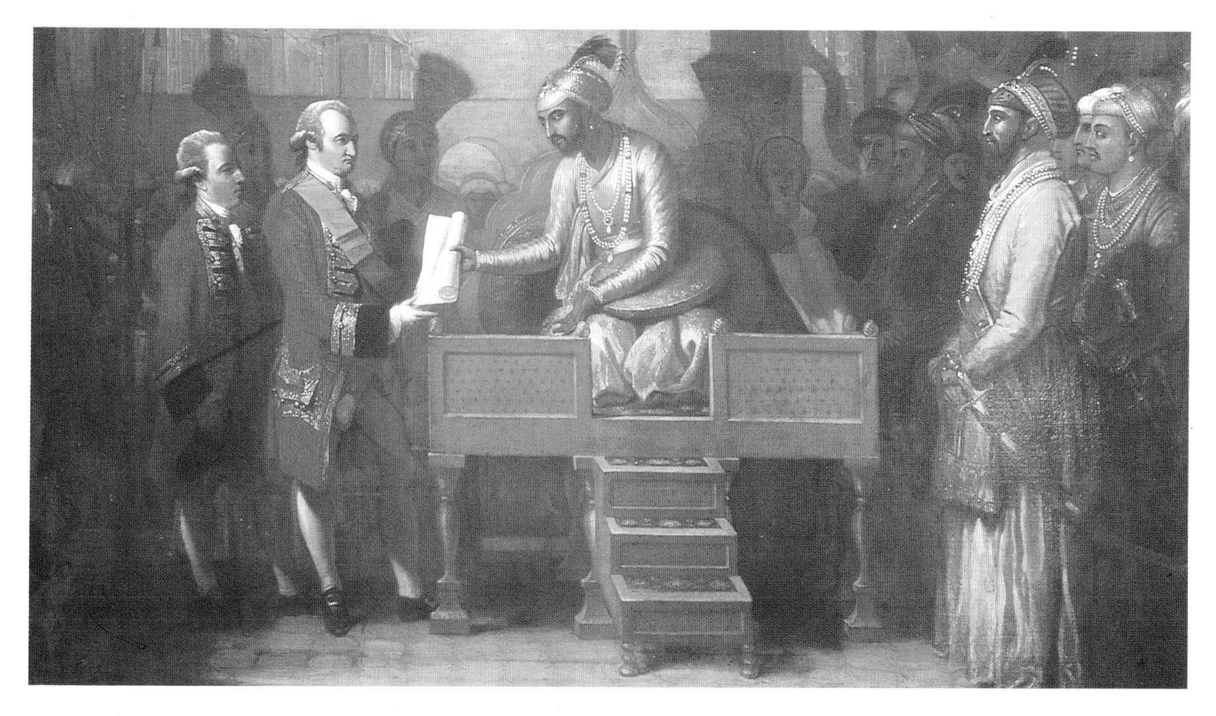

Robert Clive receives documents from the Mughal emperor which grant Britain the right to collect revenues in the 1750s. Direct rule followed in 1858 and Victoria was crowned Empress of India in 1877.

Queen Victoria

Above: **Victoria (1837-1901) was only 18 when she came to the throne and needed guidance from her first prime minister, Lord Melbourne. She went on to be the longest reigning monarch in British history.**

VICTORIA'S REIGN saw no conflicts on the scale of the Napoleonic wars or the later world wars, but plenty of small wars broke out in this period, many of them as Britain gradually expanded its empire. Britain was not the only country to build an empire in the 19th century. France, Germany and Italy all gained territories, and Austria and Hungary had united to form the Habsburg empire. The German Reich, which means empire, was formed in 1871 when the German states of Europe, except Austria, were united. The Russian empire expanded eastwards to the Pacific Ocean; at one time it even included Alaska, which the Russians sold to America for five cents per hectare. In the Near and Middle East the Turkish Ottoman empire declined.

FAR EAST WARS

There were three Afghan wars, caused by Russian infiltration of Afghanistan; the British fought because they were anxious to stop the Russians advancing into India.

There were two Opium wars in this period fought by the British against the Chinese. The first in 1839 arose when the Chinese seized opium belonging to British merchants at Canton, in an effort to stop them trading in it. The British declared that the Chinese had no right to do this. The war ended with the Treaty of Nanking in which China gave Hong Kong to the British, who had taken it in the war. (From 1997, Hong Kong is returned to China.)

In India small wars frequently broke out as British forces defended the East India Company's possessions there. Over the years these had come more and more under the control of the British government. After the particularly bloody Indian Mutiny of 1857, all the British lands in India passed finally into government control.

THE CHARTISTS

Despite the Reform Act of 1832, the vast majority of people still had no vote – and because of this no say in the running of the country. Only men of property had the vote. Chartism was a movement calling for political reform. Its name was based on the People's Charter of 1838. Its leaders included William Lovett, Feargus O'Connor and Francis Place.

Below and below left: **Victorian men of property were influenced by the fashions worn by Prince Albert, Victoria's husband. He introduced checked and tartan trousers and black frock coats. In the 1870s women wore bustle gowns. The bustle made the back of the skirt stick out.**

The six points of the Charter were: votes for all adult males (it would be a while before women got the vote); voting by secret ballot (voting was still done in public); elections for Parliament every year; Members of Parliament (MPs) should be paid a salary and should not have to own property; and finally all constituencies (places that sent an MP to the House of Commons) should be the same size.

CHARTIST DEMONSTRATIONS

There were many Chartist demonstrations including the riots in 1839 when 24 people were killed at Newport and Birmingham. In 1848 the greatest Chartist demonstration of all assembled on Kennington Common to march across the Thames towards the Houses of Parliament. However, the bridges were sealed off by special police. Three taxi-cabs were allowed through to deliver the Chartists' petition.

Despite the peition having two million signatures of support, the movement faded because of weak leadership. But most Chartist demands were eventually met and these helped to form the parliamentary system in place today.

Below: **Planning began in the late 1840s for the Crystal Palace, a huge glasshouse built in London's Hyde Park to hold the Great Exhibition of Arts and Industry of 1851. It was organized by Prince Albert to encourage trade and progress in manufacturing techniques. The aim of the exhibition was to prove that Britain was the "workshop of the world", but foreign exhibits such as American farm machines and sewing machines, and German industrial diamonds, showed that Britain was about to be challenged in that role. The Crystal Palace was three times the size of St Paul's Cathedral. Every part of its structure was made in Birmingham.**

TIME CHART

- **1837** Eighteen-year-old Queen Victoria succeeds her uncle and reigns until 1901. Last use in England of the pillory
- **1838** Manchester merchants form the Anti-Corn Law League. First Afghan War, to check Russian infiltration (to 1842). Lord Durham sent to Canada to report after rebellion there. Working Men's Association sets up People's Charter, seeking reforms. National Gallery opened
- **1839** Parliament rejects Chartist petition: weeks of rioting follow. Anglo-Chinese Opium War begins, and lasts until 1842. W.H. Fox-Talbot invents light-sensitive photographic paper to produce photographs. Grand National first run at Aintree. Treadle bicycle invented. Turner paints *Fighting Temeraire*
- **1840** Victoria marries Prince Albert of Saxe-Coburg-Gotha. Universal penny post introduced: first adhesive postage stamps. Treaty of Waitingi with Maoris gives Britain New Zealand
- **1841** The satirical magazine *Punch* begins publication
- **1842** Mines Act bans women and children under the age of 10 from working underground. Disputed American-Canadian boundary is defined
- **1843** British forces conquer Sind, in India. Maori War: revolt against British. Thames Tunnel is opened. 474 clergy leave the Scottish General Assembly to form United Free Church of Scotland. Steamship *Great Britain* launched. William Wordsworth is appointed Poet Laureate. *News of the World* first published
- **1844** Factory Act: female workers limited to 12-hour day; 8- to 13-year olds to a 6½-hour day. Ragged School Union forms to co-ordinate schools for poor children. Rochdale Pioneers found the first Cooperative Society

THE FACTORY ACTS

Beginning in 1833, a series of 40 Factory Acts was passed by Parliament to improve conditions in the factories where most people were now working. One of the most important Acts was that of 1847, which cut working hours for women and children to 10 hours a day. This, and many other similar measures, were inspired by the seventh Earl of Shaftesbury. He is commemorated by a statue in Piccadilly Circus, London, popularly called Eros, intended to symbolize Christian charity.

Shaftesbury was also a patron of the Ragged Schools, an early attempt to provide education for poor children. It was estimated that over half the children in England and Wales could not read, though Scottish children were better educated.

Above: **The potato was the main food for most Irish people. The attack of potato blight lasted three years, during which time many starved to death or were forced to emigrate, especially to America. Many travelled in converted slave ships from Liverpool, in appalling conditions.**

THE IRISH FAMINE

Although Ireland grew large quantities of wheat and other crops, most of this food was exported to enrich absentee landlords, many of whom were living in England. About half of Ireland's eight million people survived almost entirely on potatoes.

Blight (disease) ruined the potato crop in 1845 and again in 1846, causing terrible suffering. Repeal of the Corn Laws, to allow the import of cheap corn from America, came too late to save people. The Great Famine killed almost one million Irish people, while one million more emigrated to America. The famine, and Britain's slowness to act, added to bitter Irish hatred for the British.

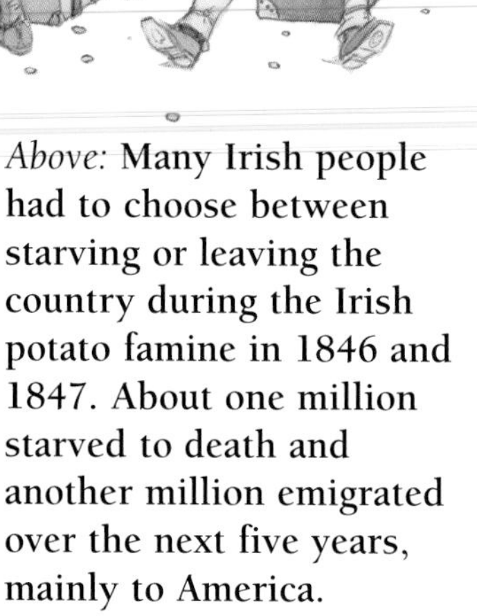

Above: **Many Irish people had to choose between starving or leaving the country during the Irish potato famine in 1846 and 1847. About one million starved to death and another million emigrated over the next five years, mainly to America.**

THE CRIMEAN WAR

The Crimean War of 1854 to 1856 was originally a conflict between Russia and Turkey. The Russians felt that the Muslim Turks had failed to deal fairly with Christians in their Balkan territories, or in the question of access to the Holy Places in Palestine. The Russians also wanted access for their warships through the Black Sea via the Bosporus and Dardanelles. Negotiations between Turkey and Russia broke down, and the two countries went to war.

- **1844** First public baths and wash houses opened in Liverpool. YMCA founded. Cheap train fares introduced. Irish Statesman Daniel O'Connell sentenced for sedition but House of Lords reverses verdict
- **1845** Maoris again rebel against the British in New Zealand. Blight wrecks Irish potato crop. Robert Thomson invents a pneumatic tyre
- **1846** Robert Peel repeals the Corn Laws. Potato failure leads to severe famine in Ireland. *Daily News* founded, with Charles Dickens as editor
- **1847** Factory Act: 10-hour day for children aged 13 to 18 and for women. Sir James Simpson uses chloroform as an anaesthetic. United Presbyterian Church of Scotland formed
- **1848** "Year of Revolutions" in Europe stimulates renewed Chartist demonstrations and petition to Parliament. Irish group led by Smith O'Brien rebel in Tipperary. Irish famine ends, but thousands emigrate to America. Public Health Act improves sanitation
- **1850** Tenant Right League founded in Ireland. Britain buys Gold Coast forts from Denmark. Local authorities empowered to start public libraries
- **1851** Window Tax abolished. The Great Exhibition is held
- **1852** British annex part of Burma. Britain gives New Zealand a new constitution
- **1853** Queen Victoria has chloroform for birth of eighth child. Smallpox vaccination compulsory. Crimean War: Britain, France, Turkey, Piedmont-Sardinia against Russia
- **1854** Siege of Sevastopol; Florence Nightingale pioneers modern nursing
- **1855** Fall of Sevastopol. *Daily Telegraph* first published

Britain and France feared Russia expanding her territory, and sent their fleets into the Black Sea to protect Turkish coasts, and were quickly allied on Turkey's side. The kingdom of Piedmont-Sardinia later joined the conflict against Russia.

Above: **The charge of the Light Brigade in 1854, during the battle of Balaclava in the Crimean War where the French and British fought the Russians. The battle was won by the British. But owing to the confusion of their officers, nearly 250 of 673 men in the Light Brigade were killed or wounded during this misjudged charge.**

SIEGE OF SEVASTOPOL

Forces from Britain, France and Piedmont-Sardinia landed in the Crimea and besieged the Russian fortress of Sevastopol (also known as Sebastopol) in 1854. The allies were badly supplied and managed but they won three battles against the Russians, at the Alma River, Balaclava, and Inkerman. The Russians were held back because a lack of railways prevented supplies and reinforcements from getting through. Disease and bad weather took a fearful toll of both sides. Eventually the besieged city of Sevastopol fell to the allied troops, and soon afterwards peace was made. The Turks guaranteed the rights of Christian subjects, and Russia was forced to give up some small amounts of territory.

Left: **The Victoria Cross is the highest decoration in Britain. It was instituted by Queen Victoria in 1856 and first awarded during the Crimean War. It is awarded to members of the British and the Commonwealth armed forces for exceptional gallantry in the presence of the enemy. It consists of a bronze Maltese cross on a crimson ribbon with an inscription saying *For Valour.***

Medicine

The cholera epidemic of 1854 killed 52,293 people, while one in 1848-1849 killed 72,000. These outbreaks spurred people to fight the disease by improving sanitation, especially in the bigger cities. The creation of modern sanitation was supported by a network of associations in which politicians, medical men and social scientists worked together to bring about reforms.

It was during the Crimean War that Florence Nightingale made a name for herself as the nurse who developed methods of sanitation and cleanliness in military hospitals. The British, lacking any other heroes in the Crimean War, acclaimed Florence Nightingale as a national heroine.

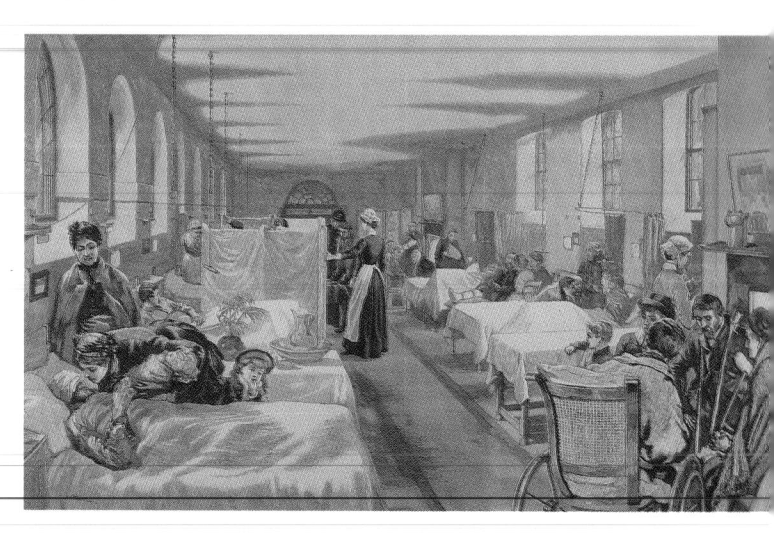

Above: **The accident ward in Guy's Hospital, London on a visiting day in 1887. The work of Florence Nightingale and Joseph Lister made people realize that by killing germs they were killing disease.**

THE FIRST MODERN SEWERS

In London the work improving sanitation was entrusted to the engineer Sir Joseph Bazalgette. His task was to provide a system of sewers which would not only drain off surface rainwater, but also take household sewage: at that time householders were forbidden to discharge their waste into the sewers, and had to use cess pits, which were emptied perhaps once every year. Bazalgette constructed five major sewers, into which a network of smaller ones flowed. One of the main sewers runs under the Embankment. The Embankment was specially built to disguise the sewers. Bazalgette's sewers have remained in use for over a century.

FOCUS ON FLORENCE NIGHTINGALE

Florence Nightingale (1820-1910) founder of modern nursing, was born of wealthy parents in Florence, Italy. She trained as a nurse against their wishes. In 1860, Florence Nightingale founded the first training school for nurses in London after the terrible sights she and her 38 nurses saw during the Crimean War (1854-1856). There the wards were filthy, with unwashed, blood-stained beds. Medical supplies, food and bedding consistently failed to arrive. Florence Nightingale took charge and by the end of the war had saved many lives. She died in 1910 aged 90.

PUBLIC HEALTH

Edwin Chadwick helped to create a Board of Health in London with the power to set up local boards in areas where death rates were exceptionally high. The boards organized street cleaning, the building of pavements and the development of proper sewers. Slowly, decent sanitation, public water supplies and street lighting (first gas then electric) were to be found even in the poorest areas of Victorian cities.

HOSPITALS

In the 19th century, life expectancy increased more from public health improvements than from medical discoveries. Throughout the 1800s the death rate in the cities far exceeded that in rural areas. The building of modern hospitals was important: Great Ormond Street Children's Hospital opened in 1852, and Broadmoor was built for the criminally insane in 1862.

In 1899 the School of Tropical Medicine was started. Medical pioneers Manson and Ross identified the mosquito that carried malaria, which was of significant benefit to people in the British colonies.

Left: **The British surgeon Joseph Lister (1827-1912) radically reduced the risk of infection during operations by using antiseptics. He used a solution of carbolic acid to clean wounds and to scrub surgeons' hands. He also pioneered the practice of sterilizing instruments.**

VACCINATION

Edward Jenner (1749-1823) was an English doctor who helped to make people immune to smallpox. At this time the disease killed one in ten people, mostly children. Jenner noticed that dairy maids never seemed to catch smallpox. But they did catch a milder form of the disease called cowpox from the cows.

In 1796 Jenner took cowpox from the infected finger of a dairy maid and injected a volunteer 8-year-old boy with tiny amounts of the virus. This caused the disease to stimulate the body's natural defences. The word vaccine comes from the Latin *vacca*, meaning cow. When Jenner injected the boy with the smallpox virus later, no disease developed. Free vaccination was made available in 1840. By the 1880s smallpox had been virtually wiped out in England.

PAINKILLERS

Another important step for modern medicine was the use of anaesthetics (painkillers). In the 1840s, a Scottish doctor, Sir James Simpson (1811-1870) put patients under chloroform vapour to ease childbirth pains. Queen Victoria was given it during the birth of her eighth child.

ANTISEPTICS

In the 1860s Joseph Lister (1827-1912) worked to combat the dangers of wound infections. From reading Louis Pasteur's work on how infections came from germs, Lister developed chemical disinfectants to make everything that came into contact with a wound antiseptic (or germ free). Lister began to practice antiseptic surgery in Glasgow in 1865.

Such advances in science and medicine laid the foundations for modern medical practises; for example, vaccination was later used to fight cholera, typhoid fever, tetanus and polio.

Microscope

Thermometer

Early syringe

Stethoscope

Syringe

Artificial hand

Lister's carbolic acid

Left: **Some of the medical appliances and instruments used today date from earlier eras: the microscope was invented in 1590, thermometers in the 1600s. Lister's carbolic spray disinfected the air during operations thus reducing death after surgery.**

CHARLES DARWIN

Charles Darwin, born in England in 1809, became one of the world's most famous naturalists. He developed his theory of evolution, largely from observations of nature made during a five-year voyage on HMS *Beagle*. Darwin set off in 1831 to Tahiti, New Zealand Australia and South America. The Galapagos Islands lie about 1,610 kilometres off the coast of South America and home to animals found nowhere else. Here he observed that these animals had adapted and evolved to survive.

In 1859, Darwin finally published his theory in his book *On the Origin of Species*. At first his theory met with great opposition, especially from the Church, and he was ridiculed by cartoonists. Today much of his thesis is widely accepted. Darwin died in 1882 and was buried in Westminster Abbey in London.

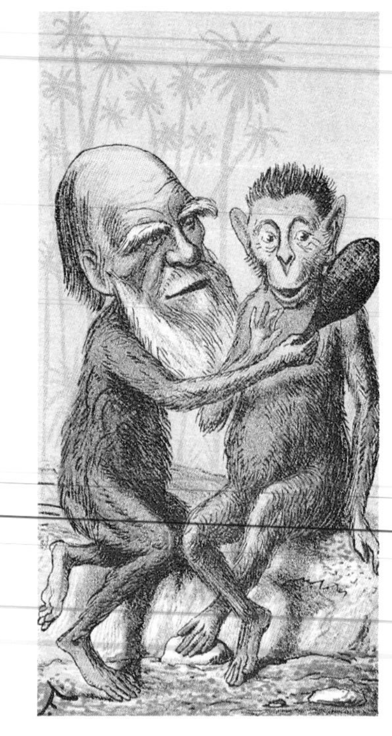

Above: **A newspaper cartoon making fun of Darwin's misunderstood proposal that all people are descended from apes. His theory of evolution upset many people.**

THE INDIAN MUTINY

By 1850, 200 million people of India remained under the rule of the East India Company that Robert Clive had help to secure in the 1750s. The Company had started as a trading concern but had turned into a government, ruling a huge area with people who had different religions and languages.

- **1855** Chemist Alexander Parkes invents xylonite (early form of celluloid). Dried milk powder invented. London sewers modernized. YWCA founded. Missionary David Livingstone discovers the Victoria Falls in Africa
- **1856** Victoria Cross instituted. Treaty of Paris ends Crimean War. William H. Perkins makes first aniline dye (mauve). Big Ben cast at Whitechapel. War with Persia (to 1857)
- **1857** Anglo-Chinese War (to 1858). Indian Mutiny begins: Massacre of Cawnpore (Kanpur), relief of Lucknow. Matrimonial Causes Act: divorce courts set up in England and Wales. Albert created Prince Consort. National Portrait Gallery opens. Charles Halle founds Halle Orchestra in Manchester
- **1858** Indian Mutiny ends. Government takes over control of India from East India Company. Jews allowed to sit in Parliament and hold office. Charles Darwin and Alfred Russel Wallace announce theory of evolution of species
- **1859** Charles Darwin publishes *On the Origin of Species*; John Stuart Mill publishes *On Liberty*; Samuel Smith publishes *Self Help* – manual on how to succeed. Scottish National Gallery opened
- **1860** Second Maori War in New Zealand. Last bare-knuckle boxing match in England: 42-round draw. First modern Welsh Eisteddfod. British Open Golf Championship begins

Left: **During the Indian Mutiny bitter fighting took place in the cities of Delhi, Cawnpore and Lucknow. The rebellion ended in 1858 because the rebels were not united.**

There were a number of causes for the Indian Mutiny in 1857. Among them was the belief among the sepoys (Indian soldiers) that the British could not have much real power because the army of Bengal comprised five native soldiers to every British one. Also several British reforms imposed upon Indians interfered with their traditional customs, such as banning *suttee*. In this Indian custom, widows would lie on their husbands' funeral pyres to die with them. British authorities also objected to the custom of the throwing of babies into the River Ganges.

The flashpoint for the mutiny was the issue of new Enfield rifles with cartridges greased with animal fat. The sepoys had to bite the ends off the cartridges, and so taste the fat: this went against both Hindu and Muslim religions. The Indian government gave orders that no cow or pig fat was to be used, but the sepoys were not reassured. On May 10, 1857, sepoys at Meerut, 65 kilometres north of Delhi, shot their British officers and moved up the river until they captured Delhi. The mutiny spread quickly throughout the Bengal army.

BRITAIN TAKES DIRECT CONTROL

The mutiny continued with the massacre of British prisoners by mutineers, and the bloody revenge taken by the British, as well as the Sikhs who supported them, when suppressing the revolt. As a result of the mutiny, the British government took control of India from the commercially-minded directors of the East India Company, and thoroughly reorganized the Indian army.

Right: **Big Ben is the name given to the bell in the clock tower of the Houses of Parliament. The bell was cast in 1858 and nicknamed after Sir Benjamin Hall who was responsible for supervising the building. The tower was completed two years later.**

CONVICTS SENT TO AUSTRALIA

In 1868, the punishment of transportation, which began in the reign of Elizabeth I, ended. It was an extension of the older punishment of banishment or exile. The British had established penal, or punishment, settlements in North America to which convicts could be sent. After the American War of Independence, North America could no longer be used for transportation, so Australia was opened up as a new place for penal colonies. More than 174,000 convicts were shipped over mainly to Sydney to spend their sentence in work gangs, for periods varying from a few years to life. Many convicts settled there after their release. Settlers and Aborigines fought over the land and many Aborgines were killed.

Left: **A chain-gang of prisoners in 1831 returning from their hard labour in Hobart, Tasmania, an island off the south coast of Australia. Transportation to new colonies, often for life, was punishment for many criminals until 1868.**

Feats of Engineering

MANY OF THE DEVELOPMENTS in factory production methods, transport, and communications and the growth of urban areas, which we call the Industrial Revolution, took part before the Victorian era, from the 1750s onwards. But these developments gathered pace in the mid-1800s.

The roads at the time of the Industrial Revolution could not cope with the heavy loads of coal and iron urgently needed by the new industries. The easiest way to move such loads was by water. The solution was to dig canals, which were known as "navigations" at the time. Britain's new canal network began in 1757 with the Sankey Navigation, which linked St Helen's coalfield to the Mersey River, and ended in 1847 with the Caledonian Canal in Scotland.

Above: **The Victorian engineer, Isambard Kingdom Brunel, designed the Clifton Suspension Bridge which spans the Avon Gorge near Bristol. It is 75 metres high and was erected in 1864.**

Below: **Brunel completed the *Great Eastern* in 1858. It was an enormous passenger ship for its time with berths for 4,000 passengers. This ship measured 211 metres long and 26 metres wide.**

COMMUNICATIONS SPEED UP

Roads and railroads had also become more efficient. Not long before Victoria's accession to the throne, Thomas Telford and John Macadam made well-surfaced, level roads that were inexpensive. A journey by stagecoach from London to Edinburgh might have taken two weeks in 1745, but took only two and a half days by the early 1800s.

During the 1840s trains became the chief form of transport for passengers, freight, post and newspapers – which helped to speed up a revolution in communications. By 1879, trains could average 96.5 kilometres per hour, and cut travelling time even further. A journey which would have taken 20 hours by stagecoach took under seven hours by train.

TRANSATLANTIC TRAVEL

Sea transport was revolutionized by steamships. During the late 1800s, shipbuilders began to use steel rather than iron mainly because steel ships were stronger and lighter than ships constructed of iron. Isambard Kingdom Brunel was an early and major contributor to iron and steam transport. As a highly gifted and imaginative engineer he also built many tunnels and bridges, for example, the Clifton

Suspension Bridge at Bristol. Brunel built the largest iron ship of its time in 1843, the *Great Britain*. In 1970 it was rescued as a rusting hulk from the Falkland Islands and towed back to Bristol Docks where it was fully restored. Brunel also introduced the broad gauge railway (with tracks about two metres apart). This was later abandoned for a narrower standard gauge.

The effects of the travel revolution by steamer and steam train during the 19th century can be compared to the way the telephone, television and transport by air changed the way we lived from the 1960s.

In just 40 years since the opening of the first public railway from Stockton to Darlington in 1826, a rail network linked all the major towns in Britain. Many cities showed off impressive public stations, such as St Pancras in London, which was combined with a hotel and was designed by Gilbert Scott. The first *Railway Time Tables* were also completed in the 1860s.

THE POST ARRIVES

It was not only passengers who benefitted from this new cheap and quick way to travel. In 1840 the first adhesive postage stamp was introduced – the Penny Black – and in 1855 came the first letter boxes, called pillar boxes, in London. The post was at first carried by stagecoach but the new postal service soon came to rely on the quicker and cheaper transport of the railways.

Above: **Many Victorian railway stations were grand buildings with elaborate ironwork and delicately carved wood.**

Above: **Isambard Kingdom Brunel (who lived from 1806 to 1859) was not only the engineer behind the Great Western Railway but was also responsible for three steamships and several dockyards.**

- **1861** Civil War breaks out in US. Trent affair: US warship seizes Confederate emissaries on British ship; clash narrowly avoided. Prince Consort dies of typhoid. Paper duties repealed. Mrs Beeton publishes her *Book of Household Management*. Daily weather forecasts begin

- **1862** John Speke is the first European to enter Uganda. England cricket team visit Australia to play various teams. First Roman Catholic monastery in England since the Reformation founded in Suffolk

- **1863** Football Association founded. Work begins on London Underground Railway (world's first). James Clerk Maxwell suggests existence of electromagnetic waves. Broadmoor opened for criminally insane prisoners

- **1864** Britain cedes Ionian Isles to Greece. Octavia Hill begins reform of tenement buildings in London. Metropolitan Railway, London, opens. Sir Samuel White Baker discovers Lake Albert in Africa. Metric system approved in Britain for scientific work. Chimney Sweeps Act forbids use of children

- **1865** William Booth founds Christian Mission, now known as the Salvation Army

- **1866** First successful transatlantic cable. Elizabeth Garrett Anderson opens dispensary for women. Dr Barnardo opens home for orphans. Marquess of Queensberry's boxing rules adopted

- **1867** Canada becomes the first Dominion. Reform Act gives more people the vote

- **1868** Transportation to Australia ends. Benjamin Disraeli (Tory) becomes PM for the first time. Third Maori War in New Zealand. General election: William Gladstone (Liberal) becomes PM. Trades Union Congress formed

VICTORIAN BOOKS

Victorian novelists, poets and other writers reflected much more on the social changes and problems of their day than the earlier Romantic novelists like Sir Walter Scott or the poet William Wordsworth. The wretched life of the poor was described with great skill by Charles Dickens in books such as *Oliver Twist*. William Thackeray evoked an image of country and town living among the middle and upper classes in *Vanity Fair*, and Elizabeth Gaskell depicted life in the new manufacturing cities of the north in such books as *North and South*.

The strong and sometimes strict religious faith of the time was the subject of many lesser writers, especially those aiming at young readers. A typical such author was ALOE (A Lady of England, the penname of Charlotte Maria Tucker). Her highly moral tales were often given as Sunday School prizes. Anna Sewell's one book, *Black Beauty*, did much to awaken people to the cruel treatment often suffered by horses.

Above: William Wordsworth (1770-1850). His poetry was called "romantic" because it described the joys and beauties of nature.

Above: Victorian author Charles Dickens. His first stories appeared in weekly or monthly periodicals.

Left: An illustration from *Oliver Twist*, a novel written by Charles Dickens in which he portrayed the harsh conditions suffered by orphans at the time. Dickens was a keen observer of Victorian life and fiercely dedicated to social reform.

THE BRONTË SISTERS

Some of the most remarkable novels in the English language were written in this period by three sisters who lived in isolation on the Yorkshire moors. Charlotte, Emily and Anne Brontë, probably wrote to escape their oppressive surroundings, and produced thousands of poems and romantic stories involving handsome heroes and passionate women. Emily Brontë's great novel *Wuthering Heights* is still widely read today. The main character in Charlotte Brontë's *Jane Eyre*, an instant best-seller at the time and still popular, reflected women's growing spirit of independence.

THE CLIMBING BOYS

Charles Kingsley's book *The Water Babies*, described as a fairy tale, exposed a cruel 19th-century practice. Sweeps used to send little boys up chimneys to clean them. Because of the soot, the boys often suffered from breathing disorders. The book appeared in 1863, and the next year Parliament passed the Chimney Sweeps Act against this ill treatment. The practice was finally stamped out by a further, stiffer Act in 1875.

TRADE UNIONS RECOGNIZED IN LAW

The first trade unions, or combinations, came into existence early in the 1700s as the Agricultural and later the Industrial Revolution completely changed the way labourers worked. Unions ran into trouble in 1799 when they were officially banned because it was feared they might encourage the workers to revolt. This was at a time when the violent excesses of the French Revolution were still very much on people's minds. This ban was lifted in 1824, and after that unions grew rapidly, as did strikes against the payment of poor wages and bad working conditions which were common at that time.

Some unions were ruthless in their methods: Sheffield cutlery workers were known to drop a keg of gunpowder down the chimney of a fellow worker who did not follow the union line. However, most unions were just and responsible. The Trade Union Act of 1871 finally made the unions legal, and gave them certain rights and protection for their funds. This law was passed by Parliament – the result of pressure from the newly formed Trades Union Congress.

Above: A Victorian dustman talks to a chimney sweep and his child assistant.

The Water Babies changed attitudes about sweeps using small boys to climb up sooty chimneys.

Below: This is the membership certificate of the National Union of Gas Workers and General Labourers, one of the trade unions formed in the 1880s following their legalization.

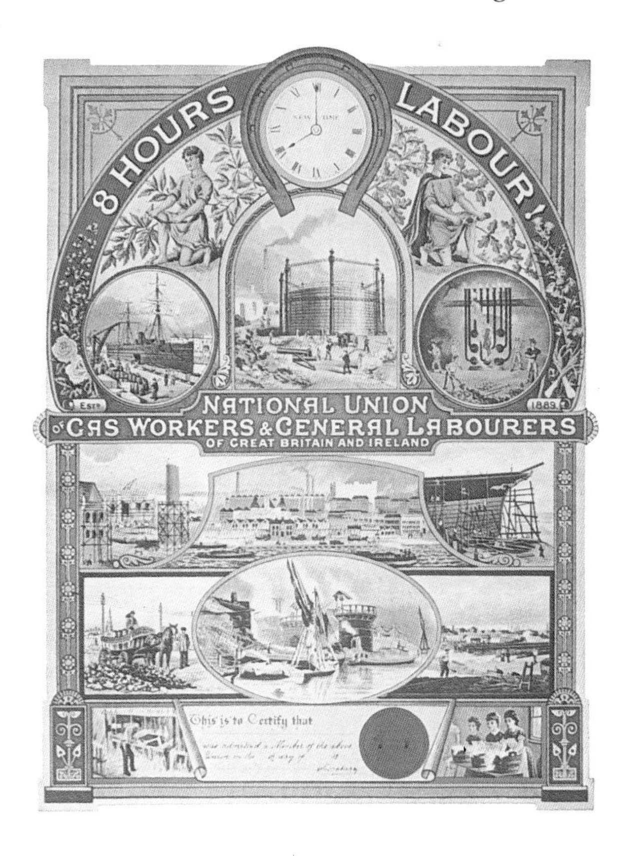

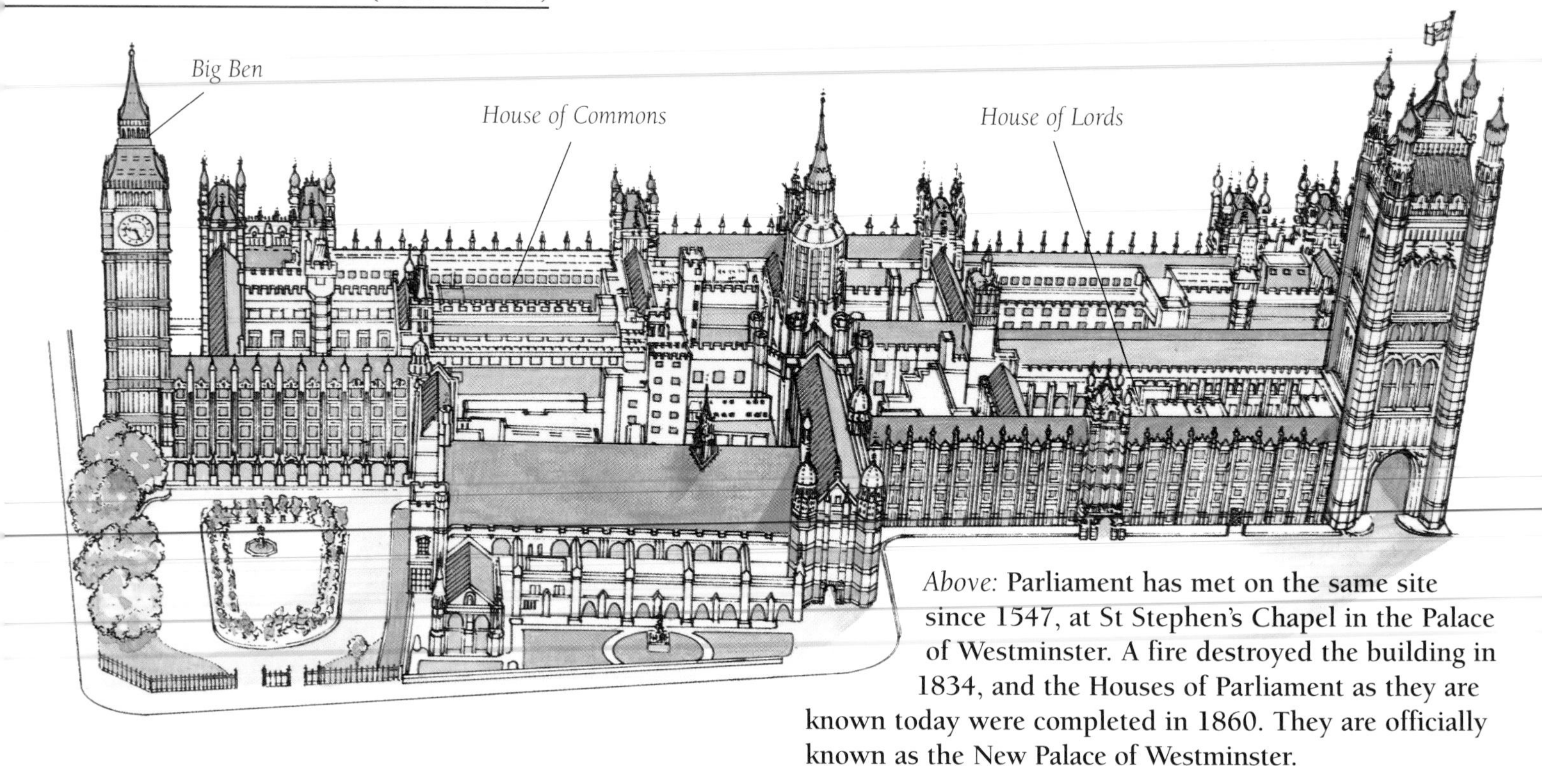

Above: **Parliament has met on the same site since 1547, at St Stephen's Chapel in the Palace of Westminster. A fire destroyed the building in 1834, and the Houses of Parliament as they are known today were completed in 1860. They are officially known as the New Palace of Westminster.**

- **1869** Irish Church disestablished. Debtors' prisons abolished. Slum clearance begins. Clipper *Cutty Sark* launched
- **1870** Married Women's Property Act gives women greater control of their own property. Education Act sets up school boards
- **1871** Local Government Boards set up in England. Trade unions formally legalized. Army reorganized: purchase of commissions abolished. Henry Stanley meets David Livingstone at Lake Tanganyika. Bank holidays introduced in England and Wales. FA Cup competition established. *Oceanic:* first large luxury liner.
- **1872** Secret ballot for elections introduced by the Ballot Act. *HMS Challenger* begins mapping the ocean bed (to 1876). First international football match, England v Scotland
- **1873** Supreme Court and Court of Appeal established. W.C. Wingfield invents game of Spharistiké (now lawn tennis)

Above: **Benjamin Disraeli (1804-1881) Conservative prime minister and outstanding political leader. He introduced several reforms and was keen to expand the empire. A witty and cultivated man, he was especially adept at dealing with Queen Victoria who could be difficult.**

THE SUEZ CANAL

When France and the Turkish rulers of Egypt undertook the construction of the Suez Canal in 1859, which opened ten years later, British traders welcomed it. However, the government opposed the canal as a threat to British trade and other links with India because it created the shortest route to India and was not controlled by Britain. Sixteen years later the spendthrift Khedive (viceroy) of Egypt was short of money, and offered his shares in the Suez Canal Company to Britain.

DISRAELI'S VISION

The prime minister, Benjamin Disraeli, wanted to expand the empire, while his political opponent and leader of the Liberal Party, William Gladstone, favoured limiting it. Disraeli was more far-seeing than his predecessors and the Foreign Office, and overruled the foreign secretary, Lord Derby, by promptly buying the Suez shares for £4 million. He borrowed the money from the international bankers, the Rothschilds, until Parliament could vote the necessary funds. The British government now owned 176,602 out of the total of 400,000 shares of the Suez Canal Company.

By this action Disraeli secured British control of the most vital trade waterway to the East. Queen Victoria gave him support for this shrewd purchase.

Left The Temperate House at the Royal Botanic Gardens, Kew, built in 1848. This structure is used to cultivate and then exchange plants with other countries. For example, tea from China was introduced as a crop to India through the work of botanists at Kew. The Palm House was built to house the exotic tropical plants that were discovered in Britain's new colonies.

KEW GARDENS

The Royal Botanical Gardens at Kew, in the London borough of Richmond, began in the 1600s with a plant collection by Lord Capel. In 1759 Princess Augusta, the mother of George III, set aside part of the gardens of Kew Palace for plant experiments, including the cultivation of rubber plants. This garden covered 3.6 hectares.

Kew Gardens continued to expand until they covered more than 117 hectares. They are dominated by a decorative pagoda designed by Sir William Chambers, which is nearly 50 metres tall, that was completed in 1762. In 1841 the gardens were handed over to the nation.

Today Kew Gardens are officially called the Royal Botanic Gardens. They are world famous as a centre of botancial studies and have the largest collection of living and preserved plants in the world. They are also important as a quarantine station for plants newly introduced to Britain and as a centre for botanical analysis.

The Princess of Wales Conservatory, opened in 1987, houses the Victorian waterlily which was introduced from South America in honour of the queen in 1837. Its leaves can be as much as two metres across.

THE RUBBER INDUSTRY

The demand for rubber grew rapidly in the 19th century, but the only source of supplies was South America. The British government decided to cultivate rubber in its newly acquired lands in the Far East. Rubber seeds were collected in Brazil and shipped to Kew Gardens, where they were raised. In 1877, 2,000 young plants were shipped to Ceylon (Sri Lanka) in special containers, and from there distributed to other countries such as Malaysia and Indonesia where the plants flourished. Today southeast Asia produces 90 percent of the world's natural rubber.

Below: The first bicycles were uncomfortable and dangerous. This Matchless bicycle made in 1883 was nicknamed the "Penny Farthing" because of its shape. It had solid rubber tyres and no brakes.

Expansion Into Africa

THE INTERIOR OF AFRICA was largely unexplored by Europeans until the 19th century. Africa was opened up by a series of British, French and German explorers. In 1788 the Association for Promoting the Discovery of the Interior Parts of Africa was set up in London, which began to send expeditions to explore the continent. Among the explorers were David Livingstone, Henry Morton Stanley, Samuel White Baker, Richard Burton and John Speke.

LIVINGSTONE THE EXPLORER

David Livingstone was born in Scotland and travelled to South Africa in 1841 to do missionary work. He made many journeys, at first with his wife and children. In 1853 he walked from the middle of Africa to the Atlantic coast. He then returned across the continent to the Indian Ocean. On his way he became the first European to see the Victoria Falls (named in honour of Queen Victoria). His second expedition was by steamboat up the Zambezi River , but it was a disaster and his wife died on the journey. He also explored the Congo River and discovered Lake Nyasa in southern Africa.

"DR LIVINGSTONE, I PRESUME"

On an expedition to find the source of the River Nile, Livingstone disappeared and was feared lost and possibly dead. In 1871, an American journalist named Henry Morton Stanley found Livingstone alive at Ujiji on the shores of Lake Tanganyika. Stanley approached Livingstone with the immortal words: "Dr Livingstone, I presume". Livingstone died in 1873 and is buried in Westminster Cathedral.

THE ZULU WAR

Britain was involved in two wars in southern Africa in three years. The Zulu War began when a large Zulu army of 40,000 men under King Cetewayo threatened the Transvaal. The Boers (farmers) of the Transvaal sought British protection. In the middle of January 1879, the local commander sent a force into Zululand, only to have it massacred by the Zulus. Reinforcements from Britain had to be brought in to subdue the Zulus.

Above: **The missionary Dr Livingstone explores the Zambezi River. In the mid-1800s he made a number of expeditions into the African interior.**

Below: **Until 1880 most of Africa was independent. But by 1914 European nations had divided it up between them and claimed areas as their colonies.**

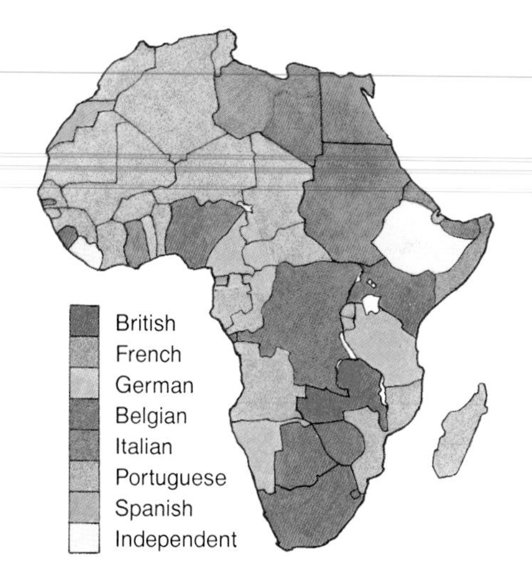

THE FIRST BOER WAR

In April 1880, Gladstone's Liberal government took power. The First Boer War broke out when the Boers (descendants of Dutch settlers) of the Transvaal formed the idea that they might persuade the new British Ministry to give them back their independence, which they had surrendered when they sought British aid against the Zulus. On December 16, 1880, the Boers, under the leadership of Paul Kruger, proclaimed their independence. After they defeated the British at Majuba Hill in 1881, the independence of the Transvaal was again recognized by Gladstone's government, though the British kept control of its foreign policy.

Above: **The Zulus are a tribe of South Africa. They defeated British troops at the battle of Isandhlwana in the Zulu War of 1879. They lost the battle of Rorke's Drift and the British won the war.**

THE SCRAMBLE FOR AFRICA

After 1870 more and more colonies were established by Britain. British governments were especially concerned to take over large parts of Africa before their rivals. Britain and France were first in what became called the "scramble for Africa" – a race to acquire colonies. Other colonial powers included Italy, Germany, Spain, Belgium and Portugal.

The European powers held a conference in 1884 and 1885 to divide Africa between them. The British gained colonies on the coasts of both west and east Africa. On the west coast they colonized Gambia, Sierra Leone, the Gold Coast and Nigeria. On the east coast they took control of Uganda and Kenya. By 1902, there were only two independent African countries left, Ethiopia and Liberia.

Right: **European heads of state attended a conference in Berlin in 1884 to decide who controlled the various parts of the African continent. They drew lines across a map of Africa to stake their claims. Native Africans were not consulted or given any say in what happened to their countries.**

- **1874** Conservatives win election: first clear majority since 1841. Britain annexes Fiji
- **1875** Public Health Act: rules for sanitation for all house-owners. Britain buys shares in Suez Canal. Plimsoll Line introduced to stop overloading of ships: it consists of a line drawn on the outside of a ship, which is not allowed to go below the water line. Artisans' Dwellings Act: local councils empowered to clear slums. Food and Drugs Act controls the substances added to food. Matthew Webb becomes first man to swim the English Channel. Gilbert and Sullivan produce their first opera: *Trial by Jury*
- **1876** Benjamin Disraeli becomes Earl of Beaconsfield. Grey squirrel introduced from US. Queen Victoria is proclaimed Empress of India.
- **1877** Britain annexes Walvis Bay and the Transvaal in South Africa. First Wimbledon championships
- **1878** The formation of the Irish National Land League. Electric street lighting in London. First British telephone company. William Booth names his mission the Salvation Army. Red Flag Act: steam road vehicles limited to 6.4 km/h, and required to be preceded by a man with a red flag as a warning
- **1879** Zulu War. Afghans murder British legation: Britain invades Afghanistan. Worst crop failure of the century. London's first telephone exchange. First railway dining-car in Britain. Tay Bridge collapses in gale. William Crookes develops the cathode ray tube (essential part of early televisions)
- **1880** Flogging abolished in Royal Navy

VICTORIA WITHOUT ALBERT

The young Victoria, aged 21, was married to her German cousin Albert in 1840, having proposed to him in 1839. On her marriage to Albert, Victoria stopped calling herself a Hanoverian and became a Saxe-Coburg after her husband's family.

Prince Albert died from typhoid fever in 1861 and Queen Victoria went into a deep and apparently permanent mourning. Every night Albert's clothes were laid out on his bed at Windsor, and every morning fresh water was placed in the basin in his room. The queen kept a photograph of Albert above her bed. Although she dealt with ministers and state papers as dutifully as before, she made few public appearances, refusing even to open Parliament each year. She was nicknamed "the Widow of Windsor". In the late 1870s the prime minister Benjamin Disraeli persuaded Victoria to return to public life. After her Golden Jubilee in 1887, when she celebrated 50 years on the throne, she was seen in public more often. Victoria died in 1901.

THE BRADLAUGH CASE

In English law, an oath is an appeal to God to witness the truth of a statement. To help people whose religion forbids them to take oaths, the law allows affirmation – a solemn declaration of truth. But when the free thinker Charles Bradlaugh was elected a Member of Parliament it was found that the rules of the House of Commons did not allow affirmation, and he was excluded.

Bradlaugh offered to take the oath, but was again excluded on the grounds that as he was a free thinker the oath would not be binding. His constituents re-elected him three times, and each time he was ejected from the House, on one occasion by ten policemen. Finally, in 1886, the Speaker of the House of Commons ruled that he could take the oath. As a Member of Parliament, Bradlaugh persuaded the Commons to change the rules to allow affirmation to prevent other free thinkers from being excluded.

JACK THE RIPPER

Victorian London was rocked by the horror of the crimes committed by Jack the Ripper. He committed a series of at least seven gruesome murders in the Whitechapel district in 1888. The ripper's victims were all prostitutes and were all killed in a similar way. Many attempts were made to catch the killer. At one stage a victim's eyes were photographed in the vain hope that the image of the killer would be seen on her retina. But the case remains one of Britain's most famous unsolved crimes.

Right: **A double-decker electric tram which became a popular form of city transport during the late Victorian era. Public trams, and later buses, gave ordinary people the opportunity to travel cheaply and easily across towns for the first time.**

KEIR HARDIE

Keir Hardie was one of the leading figures in the formation of the Labour Party. Hardie had a tough upbringing. He never went to school, but from the age of ten worked in the Lanarkshire mines. The only formal education he had was at night school. Hardie learned public speaking from temperance, or anti-alcohol meetings and became an active trade unionist and a journalist. In 1888 he founded the Scottish Parliamentary Labour Party. In 1892 he was elected Independent Socialist MP for West Ham, and a year later started the Independent Labour Party (ILP). A few years later he helped to establish the Labour Representation Committee, which became the modern Labour Party.

Above: **The first electric underground railway, or subway, was opened in London in 1890. Steam trains had been used on underground lines in London since 1863. This underground system soon became known as the "tube".**

LONDON'S UNDERGROUND RAILWAY

London's underground system was the world's first. It was suggested by Charles Pearson, a city solicitor, as part of the improvement plans which followed the opening of the Thames Tunnel in 1843. It took Parliament a long time to accept the idea of a railway system under the streets of London.

However in 1853 and 1854 the Commons passed a bill approving the construction of the Metropolitan District Railway, an underground line which was to run between Farringdon Street and Bishop's Road, Paddington. It was to be just over six kilometres long.

Work began in 1860, and the line was opened to passengers on January 10, 1863. The trains were steam locomotives that burned coke as fuel, and getting rid of the smoke from under the ground proved to be a major problem. The first electric underground railway opened in 1890, charging 2d (two old pence) on any journey on the 4.8 kilometre City and Southwark Subway line.

- **1880** Relief of Distress Act for Ireland. Employers' Liability Act. Education up to age 13 becomes compulsory. Transvaal declares independence
- **1881** Transvaal Boers defeat the British at Majuba Hill, who recognize their independence. Land Act attempts to give fairer deal to Irish tenants. Charles Stewart Parnell MP, and others jailed for opposing the Act. Flogging abolished in the army. Postal orders first issued. Benjamin Disraeli dies
- **1882** Phoenix Park murders: Fenians kill Lord Frederick Cavendish, chief secretary for Ireland, and Thomas Burke, permanent under-secretary. British troops crush revolt in Egypt. Preliminary work on Channel Tunnel begins
- **1883** Irish terrorists try to blow up *The Times* office in London. Royal Red Cross Order founded
- **1884** Third Reform Bill: electorate increased to 5,000,000. Fabian Society founded. Work starts on *New English Dictionary*, which takes until 1928 (now the *Oxford English Dictionary*). Charles Parsons makes first practical steam turbine generator

Below: **In 1897 Queen Victoria celebrated her Diamond Jubilee – 60 years on the throne. She drove in an open carriage from Buckingham Palace to St Paul's Cathedral. Cheering crowds lined the streets.**

Rhodes in Africa

ONE OF THE MOST INFLUENTIAL men in the history of southern Africa was Cecil Rhodes. A parson's son, he went to Natal from England at the age of 17 because his health was poor. He made a fortune in the Kimberley diamond mines, while paying frequent visits to Oxford to study for a degree. When gold was discovered in the Transvaal, Rhodes made another fortune. He went into politics, and by 1890 was Premier of Cape Colony. He acquired the rights to develop Matabeleland and Mashonaland and formed them into the colony of Rhodesia (now Zimbabwe and Zambia).

THE JAMESON RAID

Rhodes was eventually brought down by his friend, Dr Leander Starr Jameson. Jameson led an armed raid, comprising police from the British South Africa Company, into the Transvaal to try to overthrow the Boer government, which was denying voting and other rights to the *Uitlanders*, or foreign workers, in the gold fields. Jameson's attack failed. Rhodes was blamed for the raid, and had to resign as Premier of the Cape. Jameson, after a jail sentence in Britain, returned to Cape Colony and became its Premier. Rhodes died in 1902 aged 49. He left his wealth to create Rhodes Scholarships to Oxford University, for Commonwealth, German and American students.

Above: **A *Punch* magazine cartoon of Cecil Rhodes showing him straddling the African continent like a giant, just as the Colossus of Rhodes had straddled the harbour of Rhodes in Ancient Greece.**

THE SECOND BOER WAR

The Second Boer War from 1899 to 1902 followed from the Jameson Raid of 1895, and had much the same cause. Britain supported the political rights of the *Uitlanders* (foreign workers), which the Boer rulers of the Transvaal refused to recognize. Thousands of the *Uitlanders* were British, and they sent a petition to Queen Victoria asking for help. Prolonged talks broke down, and the Boers declared war. They were supported by the Orange Free State, which was also Boer-governed.

THE RELIEF OF MAFEKING

The Boers, who greatly outnumbered the British, invaded Cape Colony and laid siege to the towns of Kimberley, Ladysmith and Mafeking. Mafeking was defended by Colonel Robert Baden-Powell, later renowned as the founder of the Boy Scout movement. In 1900, when the 200-day-long siege of Mafeking ended, rejoicing in London was so extreme that a new verb was coined: to *maffick*, or rejoice riotously.

Reinforcements were sent from England, and gradually the British conquered the country, though the Boers carried on a guerrilla campaign for another 18 months. Boer farms were burned and large groups of Boer women and children were sent to prison camps known as concentration camps, the first use of the term.

Right: **Christ Church College, Oxford. The first Rhodes Scholars came to Oxford in 1904. About 90 scholarships are awarded each year. US President Bill Clinton was a former Rhodes Scholar.**

Above: **British troops attack a Boer stronghold. The Boers had commando units who were highly trained and armed and brilliant riders. Whole families fought vigorously to defend their freedom.**

The peace treaty of Vereeniging in 1902 ended the war by annexing Transvaal and the Orange Free State, but promised them self-government, which they were given in 1907.

POPULAR REFORMS

Politics in the later part of Queen Victoria's reign were dominated by William Gladstone who served four terms as prime minister. Victoria did not get on as well with Gladstone as she had with Disraeli. Unlike Disraeli, Gladstone was not interested in expanding the British Empire. He was more concerned about making and passing laws which would help to bring about socal reform at home. In 1876 he helped to amend the Parliamentary Reform Bill and doubled the number of people able to vote. For the first time the vote was extended to almost all the working classes including two million agricultural labourers. Women, however, still had no vote.

Right: **Robert Baden-Powell (1857-1941) defended Mafeking in the Boer War. He became a national hero, and went on to found the Boy Scout movement in 1908.**

- **1885** The Mahdi revolts in Sudan: British Governor General Charles Gordon slain at Khartoum. First Secretary of State for Scotland appointed. Francis Galton proves that each person's fingerprint is unique

- **1886** British annex Upper Burma. Irish Home Rule Bill defeated. Liberals split: some form Liberal Unionist Party. Severn Tunnel opened. Tilbury Docks, Essex, opened

- **1887** Queen Victoria's Golden Jubilee. Britain annexes Zululand. Bloody Sunday: Trafalgar Square protest over jailing of Irish nationalist William O'Brien. Coal Mines Act: no boys under 13 allowed to work underground

- **1888** County Councils established. John Boyd Dunlop re-invents the pneumatic tyre. *The Financial Times* first issued. Football League is founded. Jack the Ripper murders prostitutes in Whitechapel. London Miners' Federation founded

Above: **A cartoon in the magazine *Punch* of April 15, 1876. It shows Queen Victoria being offered the Imperial Crown of India, "the jewel in the crown", by the prime minister, Benjamin Disraeli.**

Below: **The Esplanade at Calcutta in the heyday of the British Empire. It was the capital of British India from 1773-1912 and many imposing buildings were built there in European style.**

Gladstone also supported improvements in the provision of education. More schools were built and education finally became free and compulsory for all children up to 13 years of age.

In 1886 Gladstone became prime minister for the third time and tried to persuade Parliament to give Home Rule to Ireland. But many members of his own Liberal Party were against the Bill and it was defeated.

THE MODERN NEWSPAPER

Many newspapers read today began life in the 1800s or even earlier – the most famous being *The Times*. This paper reported Nelson's victory and death at Trafalgar, the Battle of Waterloo, and an eyewitness account of the Peterloo Massacre. Above all it brought the blunders and horrors of the Crimean War to the public's attention. *The Times* was given the nickname "The Thunderer" and was highly critical of many politicians.

Modern popular journalism was begun by Alfred Harmsworth (who became Lord Northcliffe in 1905). Sensing there was a growing demand for newspapers among the wider public, Harmsworth launched the *Daily Mail* in 1896, described at the time as "a penny newspaper for one halfpenny". In only three years it had double the circulation of any other national newspaper, and by covering popular subjects of the time such as motoring and aviation, it increased its circulation by nearly one million by the end of the century.

- **1889** Major London dock strike. London County Council set up. Secondary Education for Wales established
- **1890** Parnell sued for divorce: Liberal Party disowns him. London's first electric underground railway opened. Forth Bridge (rail) opened
- **1891** Liberals adopt programme dedicated to Home Rule for Ireland. Elementary education is made free. Leeds has Britain's first electric tramcar system
- **1892** Dam across river Vyrnwy, North Wales, to supply water to Liverpool. C.F. Cross develops viscose rayon
- **1893** Keir Hardie forms Independent Labour Party. Uganda becomes a British protectorate. Lords reject second Home Rule bill. University of Wales formed. Manchester Ship Canal completed. Liverpool overhead railway built
- **1894** Death Duties introduced. Parish councils established. James Dewar liquifies oxygen. Blackpool Tower opened
- **1895** Togoland annexed by Britain. Cecil Rhodes creates Rhodesia. London School of Economics founded. National Trust established. Westminster Cathedral begun. First Promenade Concert season. First London motor-car exhibition. Jameson Raid in Transvaal
- **1896** Fourth Ashanti War. Matabeles rebel in Rhodesia. Guglielmo Marconi patents wireless in England. Alfred Harmsworth (later Lord Northcliffe) starts the *Daily Mail*. Red Flag Act repealed: speed limit raised to 123 kph
- **1897** Victoria's Diamond Jubilee. Britain occupies Benin in protest at human sacrifices. Joseph Chamberlain's suggestion of Anglo-German alliance is poorly received

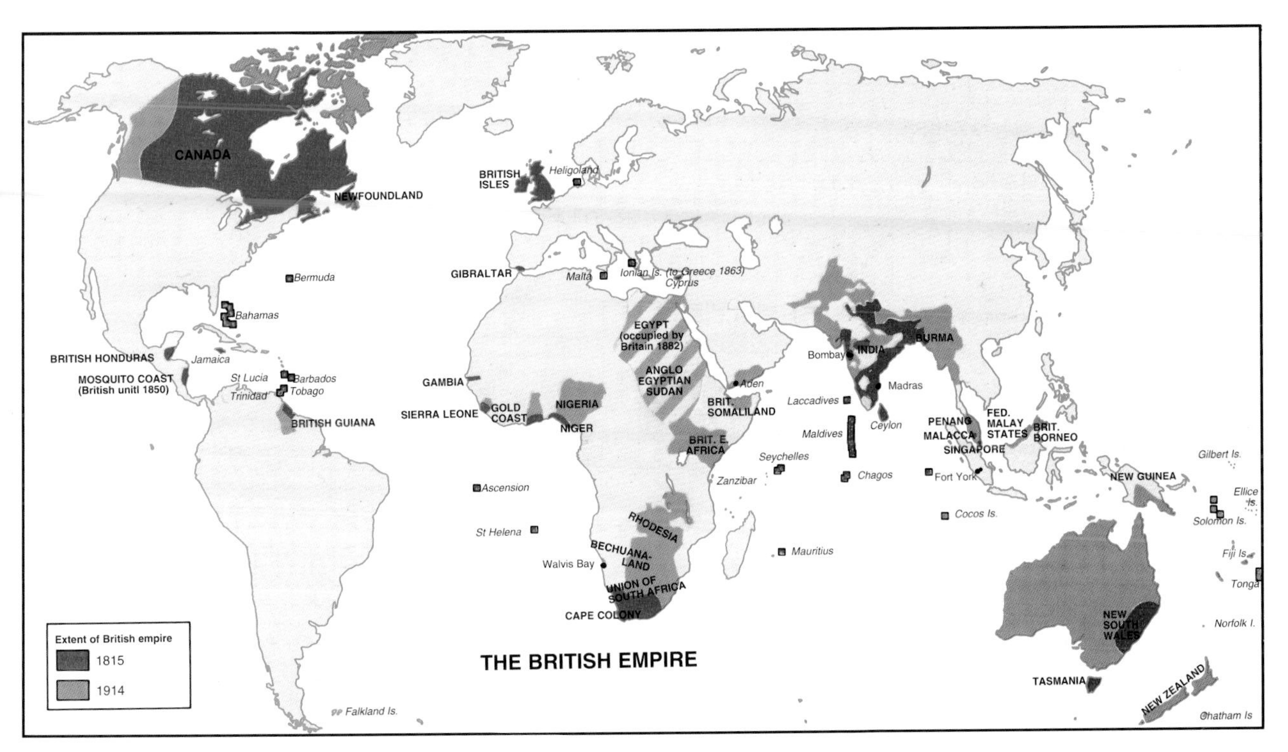

Left: **The British empire grew rapidly from 1870 to 1914 in Africa and southeast Asia. It also took hold of many key islands on trade routes including Hong Kong, Singapore, Cyprus, the Falklands, Ceylon and Gibraltar.**

Age of Empire

BY THE END OF QUEEN VICTORIA'S reign, Britain had gained more overseas lands and taken over more peoples than any other nation in history. Britain's empire included countries in every continent and islands in every ocean including colonies in the Caribbean, Africa, Asia, Australasia and the Pacific.

From the end of the Napoleonic Wars in 1815 to the start of World War I in 1914, Britain acquired so many new colonies that the empire stretched around the world. By the time Phileas Fogg made his story-book journey in *Around The World in Eighty Days* (published 1872) he could have travelled the world without having to visit an area that was not under some sort of British influence. Because the empire covered both hemispheres, it was known as "the empire on which the sun never sets".

IMPERIAL LOSS AND GAINS

Though Britain had lost the American colonies in 1783, a number of new overseas territories became part of the empire after the defeat of Napoleon in 1815. In addition, the Dutch, who had sided with the defeated French, were forced to give up lands to Britain. Britain already governed Australia as a penal colony, and had gained Canada from the French by capturing Quebec in 1759.

British naval strength was unbeatable and, for a time, "Britannia" did "rule the waves" – British boats constantly patrolled countries belonging to the British empire. The government made sure the British navy remained powerful. Britain's naval superiority was also used to maintain peace and to push forward further colonial enterprises. Strategic harbours such as Gibraltar, Hong Kong, Singapore and Aden came into British hands, and vital trading routes, such as the Cape Route (via the tip of South Africa) to India, or the Suez Canal (via Egypt) to the spice and rubber plantations of southeast Asia were also controlled by Britain.

EXPORTING BRITISH KNOW-HOW

By the 1880s, British engineers, surveyors and architects were helping to build railways, roads, bridges, factories and government buildings not only in the colonies, but also in places where Britain had influence. These people drew on the experience gained from the Industrial Revolution. Banking and investment were geared to financing the empire by trading raw materials from the colonies for home-made manufactured goods.

During the later 1800s, many people went to live and work in the colonies as traders, soldiers, engineers, diplomats and government administrators. These people took their industrial, educational and government systems with them.

Above: **Canadian fur trappers developed a profitable trade around the Hudson Bay. Among the people who emigrated to Canada were many Scottish families from the Highlands.**

India, for example, had originally been controlled by the East India Company to provided Britain with jute, tea and cotton. After British forces put down the Indian Mutiny of 1857, Parliament had to decide whether to govern India directly, or continue just to protect the trading interests of the East India Company that had been running the country. India became a colony administered by the government, as did Malaya and Burma shortly afterwards.

THE NEW DOMINIONS

By about 1900, about one-quarter of the world and its population were ruled from London and flew the Union Jack. British influence extended into mainland settlements in Central and South America and into China where it had outposts.

Queen Victoria, herself Empress of India since 1876, was a keen supporter of a foreign policy that pursued colonial expansion and upheld the empire, but not at any cost.

As more and more British and Irish people emigrated to countries within the Empire, so these lands were gradually given more freedom to govern themselves. Many colonies, notably Canada, Australia and South Africa, became known as dominions rather than colonies and allowed to govern themselves, but they still remained closely linked to Britain.

- **1897** Battle of Omdurman gives Anglo-Egyptian control of Sudan. Sale of Church livings ends. Waterloo-City Railway electrified. W. Ramsay and M.W. Travers discover neon, krypton and xenon gases
- **1899** Second Boer War begins (to 1902). London borough councils established. First motor-buses in London. First radio transmission from England to France
- **1900** Labour Representation Committee: to work for Labour group in Parliament. British relieve sieges of Ladysmith and Mafeking. Britain annexes Tonga, Orange Free State and Transvaal. Boxer Rising against foreigners in China: Britain helps suppress it. The Quaker, George Cadbury, founds Bourneville Village Trust. Arthur Evans begins excavations in Crete. *Daily Express* is founded

Below: **Winnipeg, a centre of the fur trade, was still a small town in 1870. In that year the province of Manitoba became part of the Dominion of Canada; Winnipeg became the province's capital.**

THE DOMINION OF CANADA

Canadians had become increasingly fearful that the United States might try to take them over. Canada was sparsely populated and full of natural resources. There was also the highly profitable fur trade which had been growing since the time of French explorers in the 1600s and the Hudson Bay Company in the reign of Charles II.

Several of the biggest colonies joined to form the Dominion of Canada in 1867. Each colony became a province: Quebec, Ontario, New Brunswick and Nova Scotia. The new country purchased the vast lands owned by the Hudson Bay Company. A trans-continental railway, the Canadian-Pacific, was also completed by 1885 and linked settlements across the vast area between the Atlantic and the Pacific coasts.

Left: **The expansion of the British Empire owed much to the daring and dangerous explorations of intrepid explorers all over the globe. Burke and Wills were the first white men to cross Australia. Their expedition set out in 1860 from Melbourne to the Gulf of Carpentaria but both died on their return journey. After such explorers came the settlers and later self-government. By 1890 all Australian colonies had self-government.**

THE AUSTRALIAN COMMONWEALTH

The success of the first independent dominion of Canada paved the way for the creation of a second. In 1855 the six separate Australian colonies of New South Wales, Queensland, Western Australia, Victoria, South Australia and Tasmania, had been granted self-government by Britain. They developed into democracies with elections (except for Aborigines).

The leaders of the colonies soon came to realize that some form of union was needed. None of the Australian colonies was willing to give up its individual independence, so in the end a federal form of government was agreed on. In a federal system a central government shares power with the independent regional or state governments, but is responsible for national concerns such as foreign policy. The Commonwealth of Australia finally came into being on the first day of 1901.

NEW ZEALAND

The third of the great dominions, which would eventually transform the British empire into the British Commonwealth of Nations, was New Zealand. The British government took possession of New Zealand in 1840, signing a treaty with some of the Maori chiefs and promising to protect their rights. The country had its own government from 1852, but Europeans took over Maori land and war broke out between Maoris and colonists in 1860. New Zealand troops fought bravely in the Boer War of 1899 to 1902 for Britain. Finally in 1907 New Zealand was proclaimed as a dominion, with full internal self-government. Britain retained control over defence and foreign affairs. Much of the country's progress to independence was the work of Richard Seddon, its prime minister from 1893 to his death in 1906. Seddon introduced votes for women in 1893, 25 years before Britain.

Social Change

THE INCREASE AND SUCCESS of industry meant that the middle classes grew in numbers and these people had more money to spend. People such as bank managers, factory owners and wealthy traders often built large elaborate houses to show off their wealth. We know a lot more about the people of this period because of the invention of photography from around the 1850s.

INSIDE A VICTORIAN HOME

Inside, a middle-class home the rooms would be full of over-stuffed velvet covered furniture, and heavily curtained windows often decorated with coloured glass panes. The rooms would be full of china and glass ornaments and paintings.

Below: **A big step forward in steel making was made by Henry Bessemer in 1856. In a Bessemer converter, hot air was blasted through melted iron to convert it into steel. Steel was stronger and more useful than iron. Before Bessemer's invention it had been very expensive to make.**

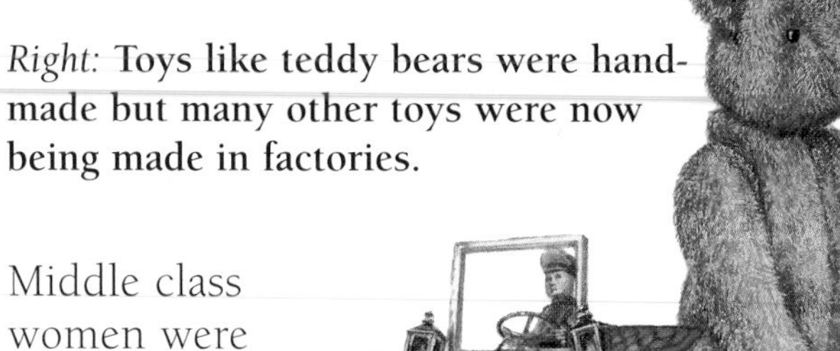

Right: **Toys like teddy bears were hand-made but many other toys were now being made in factories.**

Middle class women were expected to manage the household, with servants, including a cook and possibly a butler and coachman. They would not have a job, apart from helping charities, because it was not considered "respectable".

VICTORIAN DRESS AND LEISURE

For the wealthy, fashions reflected increasing prosperity; women wore crinolines (hooped petticoats held out over a frame of cane or whalebone) which gave their dresses a bell shape. Later, women wore a bustle at the back. Men wore frock coats and winged collars. They also had tiepins, studs, watches and chains. In the 1860s walking-sticks with silver knobs also became popular, as did patent-leather shoes and shoes laced at the front.

As the new middle classes employed servants this gave more women leisure time to try the new sports, such as archery, tennis and croquet. Children from wealthy Victorian families saw little of their parents except at tea-time. They went straight from a nursery with a nurse or nanny to a schoolroom with a governess. Their life consisted of lessons at home, walks in the park and playing with other wealthy children. They also had the first teddy bears, metal toys to play with and children's books.

PUBLIC EDUCATION

Until 1870 most children did not go to school. Most of the schools at this time were run by local churches. The Education Act in 1870 set up elected School Boards which ensured that schools were provided for children up to the age of 13 in any district which did not have a church school. The government also gave money to fund church schools. It would be another 21 years before schools became free and education compulsory, up to the age of 13.

Left, right and below: **A selection of Victorian household appliances: sewing machine; ice box (forerunner of the refrigerator); and washing machine.**

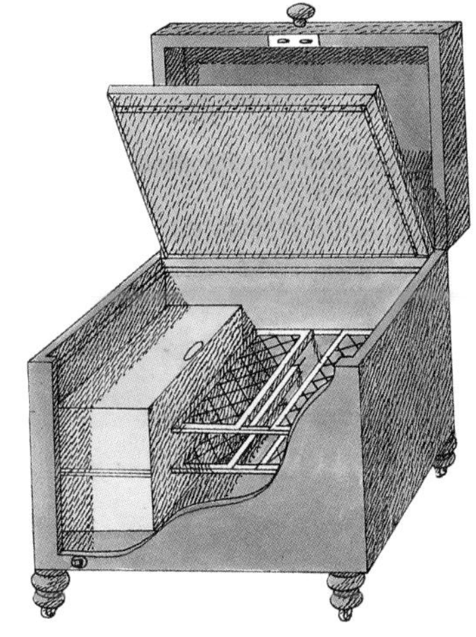

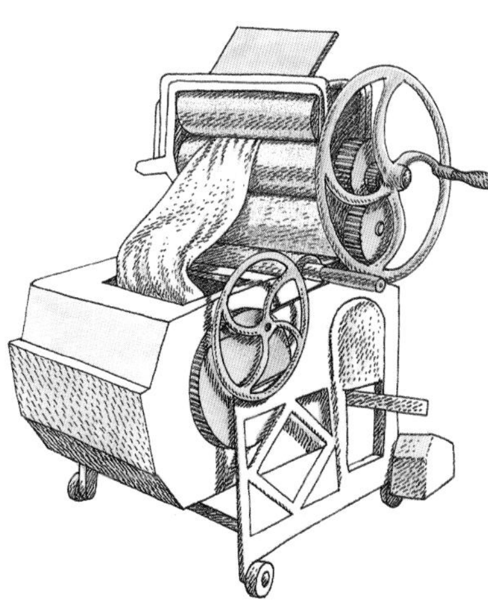

THE VICTORIAN POOR

For working class children life was very hard. Most poor children still did not go to school as they were expected to work. There was virtually no help for the unemployed, sick, old or poor at this time. People either starved, begged in the streets or were sent to the local workhouse. Here they would receive food and shelter in return for work such as breaking stones (for men) and doing laundry (for women and children).

The enormous difference between the wealthier Victorians and the poverty of the working classes stirred many social reformers to start voluntary organizations. For example Dr Barnardo founded the first of his famous homes for children in 1870. Reformers also persuaded Parliament to pass acts to improve schooling and healthcare in general and for children in particular.

In 1875 the Public Health Act attempted to make sure all houses were supplied with clean water and proper working drains. Local councils had to ensure that streets were regularly cleaned and that food sold in shops – whether cooked or raw – was clean and fit to eat.

Below: **The Salvation Army was formed by Catherine and William Booth in 1878, out of their Whitechapel Christian Mission. They offered practical help to poor people suffering from homelessness and alcoholism. It is now a worldwide organization helping those struck by poverty.**

- **1901** Queen Victoria dies; succeeded by son, Edward VII (to 1910). Anglo-Japanese Alliance signed. Balfour Education Act abolishes Board Schools. Australia becomes a Dominion. First petrol-driven motor-cycle. First British submarine launched. Marconi sends radio signal from Cornwall to Newfoundland

- **1902** Order of Merit established. Oliver Heaviside discovers ionosphere

- **1903** Britain conquers northern Nigeria. Car speed limit set at 32 km/h. Emmeline Pankhurst starts suffragette movement. First motor-taxis in London. Liverpool Cathedral begun. *Daily Mirror* founded. Universities of Liverpool and Manchester established

- **1904** *Entente Cordiale* signed. Workers' Educational Association begins. Frederick Kipping discovers silicones. J.A. Fleming invents thermionic valve. London Symphony Orchestra founded. Leeds University founded

- **1905** Automobile Association established. First public cinema shows in London. Sheffield University founded. British troops put down riot in Guyana

- **1906** Liberals win landslide election. Twenty-nine Labour MPs elected: Labour Representation Committee changes its name to Labour Party. Bakerloo and Piccadilly tube lines open in London. China and Britain agree to reduce opium production. F.G. Hopkins discovers vitamins

- **1907** New Zealand becomes a dominion. Motor-racing starts at Brooklands. Northern tube line opened. Triple Entente between Britain, France and Russia

- **1908** Herbert Henry Asquith becomes Liberal prime minister. Anglo-German tension grows. Port of London Authority set up

IMPROVED COMMUNICATIONS

Apart from the Penny Post, messages could be sent by electric telegraph and in 1858 the first transatlantic cable was laid on the bed of the Atlantic Ocean. Laying a cable on the ocean floor allowed telegraph messages to be sent between Britain and America. Scotsman Alexander Graham Bell perfected the first telephone in the late 1870s, in the United States. Britain's first telephone exchange was opened by the Telephone Company Limited. The exchange had 10 customers. By the 1890s Britain had over 45,000 telephones.

Below: **An early Marconi wireless set, with speakers and headphones. Before the wireless, sound waves were changed into electric current, sent along a wire and changed back into sound. But Guglielmo Marconi used electromagnetic waves, which travelled at the speed of light, without wires to carry sound.**

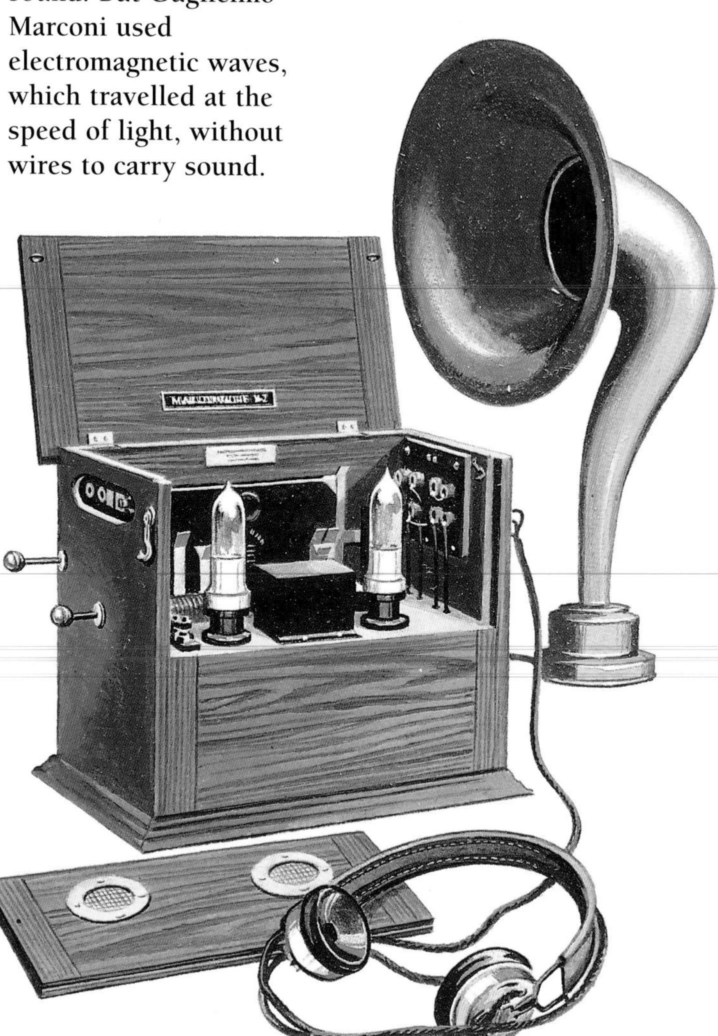

Edward VII

EDWARD, BORN IN 1841, remained Prince of Wales until he was 59. His mother, Queen Victoria, would not involve him in politics or give him any serious responsibilities. However, he did carry out many goodwill visits abroad. He became very fond of France even though Anglo-French relations were not that good. Thanks to Edward's efforts, several years of wrangling between Britain and France over overseas territories were ended by the signing of an *entente* (understanding), which became popularly known as the *entente cordiale* of 1903. The French, who had been quite hostile, were won over by the charm of Edward VII during his state visit to Paris in 1903.

Right: **Edward VII visiting his nephew, the German Kaiser Wilhelm II. Edward's peace-seeking trips to European heads of state earned him the nickname "peacemaker".**

THE EDWARDIAN ERA

Edward became king in 1901 and ruled for nine years. He was a popular king and continued to enjoy foreign travel and ceremonies, and took less interest in politics. On the surface, the Edwardian era, under a genial and pleasure-loving king, was a much brighter and more glamorous time than the closing years of Victoria's reign.

But beneath the apparent calm and settled order of things, there was growing unrest. Political strife was bitter, the Labour movement was growing in strength, women were battling for emancipation (including the right to vote) and over Europe the clouds of war were gathering.

Above: **Edward VII (1901-1910) influenced foreign affairs by making many visits to European capitals, in an attempt to calm international tensions and to prevent the outbreak of a European war.**

SCOTT OF THE ANTARCTIC

The British expedition of Robert Falcon Scott to the South Pole which took place from 1910 to 1912 ended in tragedy. On his way to Antarctica, at the age of 42, Scott heard that a Norwegian expedition led by Roald Amundsen, who was believed to be going to the Arctic, was also heading for the South Pole.

Amundsen used husky dogs to draw his sledges. Scott unwisely used ponies, which were not suited to the severe conditions and died. Snowstorms made his progress slow and difficult. Eventually Scott and four companions reached the Pole pulling their own sledges, to find that Amundsen had reached the Pole 34 days earlier.

On their way back Scott's party ran into unexpected blizzards, and died of cold and hunger only 18 kilometres from shelter and ample stores of food. Three bodies, as well as the records and diaries the men had kept, were found. Scott had written his diary up to the day of his death. News of the tragedy shook national pride.

Above: **Sheffield University, which opened in 1905, was of one of several new redbrick universities whose purpose was to broaden people's access to higher education.**

Left: **Roald Amundsen leads his huskies over the Antarctic. He reached the South Pole in December 1911, beating Robert Scott's expedition by 34 days.**

- **1908** Robert Baden-Powell founds the Boy Scout movement. Old Age Pensions for over 70s. New universities: Belfast and University of Ulster. Start of Borstal system. First aeroplane flight in Britain (Farnborough). Election of Elizabeth Garrett Anderson as first British woman mayor (Aldeburgh). The IV Olympic Games are held in London

- **1909** House of Lords reject Chancellor of the Exchequer David Lloyd George's budget proposals spark off constitutional crisis. Girl Guides established in Britain. Selfridge's store opens. A.V. Roe begins building aeroplanes in Britain. Bristol University founded. Formal opening of Victoria and Albert Museum, London

- **1910** Union of South Africa becomes a Dominion. Two general elections over budget: Liberal majority cut. Parliament Bill to curb powers of Lords: Conservative peers resist it. Edward VII dies; succeeded by son, George V (to 1936). Dr Crippen poisons his wife (body discovered seven months later). First Labour Exchanges opened. Halley's Comet observed. Louis Paulhan wins prize for London to Manchester flight. George V gives secret pledge to create enough Liberal peers to force the Parliament Bill through. Dr Crippen hanged. Mining disaster (Hulton), 350 killed

George V

George V's family name was Saxe-Coburg, which came from Prince Albert, his grandfather. For the first seven years of his reign George V kept this name. But with the outbreak of World War I against Germany, and with anti-German feeling running high, he changed his Germanic family name to Windsor. George was the second son of Edward VII (his elder brother died before him). He became king and Emperor of India at a time when Parliament was trying to limit the power of the House of Lords, and women were campaigning for the right to vote.

Left: **George V (1910-1936) held old fashioned values and with his wife, Mary, kept the monarchy popular. But the power of British monarchs had declined so much in the 19th century that by the time of George V they were little more than figureheads.**

Left: **Suffragettes in 1908 celebrate the release of two of their members from Holloway prison. Faced with the government's continued resistance to votes for women, suffragettes resorted to violence such as smashing high street shop windows and even fire-raising. But their militant methods turned some people against them. At the Derby horse race in 1913, a suffragette named Emily Davison threw herself in front of the King's horse and died from her injuries.**

VOTES FOR WOMEN

The campaign for the right of women to vote began in 1866. When an amendment to the Electoral Reform Act on female suffrage (the right to vote) was defeated, organizations were formed all over the country. In the cotton mills, women workers campaigned for the vote through trade unions and the Labour Party.

Most effective were the militant methods of the Women's Social and Political Union founded in 1903 by Emmeline Pankhurst. Its members became known as the suffragettes. These militant campaigners for votes for women tried to draw attention and support for their cause by interrupting political meetings, chaining themselves to railings and breaking windows.

SUFFRAGETTES' SUCCESS

Faced with continued resistance from the Commons who, in 1912, again rejected votes for women, the violence of the suffragette movement increased. The women resorted to arson, slashing pictures, and destroying empty property on a huge scale. These acts led to arrests and the imprisonment of many suffragettes.

In prison many women went on hunger strike, which resulted in the "Cat and Mouse" Act of 1913. This allowed prisoners to be temporarily discharged for health reasons, while making them liable for re-arrest once they had recovered. The campaign halted with the start of World War I, but women over the age of 30 finally won the vote in 1918.

THE START OF STATE WELFARE

In the 1906 election the Liberals won a landslide victory. They were supported by members of the new Labour Party who were elected to help improve the lives of working people. Herbert Asquith was prime minister and David Lloyd George, Chancellor of the Exchequer, was the driving force behind many of the reforms.

Among the reforms was the establishment of the school meal service which gave free school meals to children of parents who could not afford them. Hundreds of thousands of children now had a good meal each day – some for the first time in their lives. A free school medical service was also started so many children also saw a doctor and dentist for the first time.

Also introduced for the first time in Britain were old age pensions, labour exchanges, National Insurance and similar measures which became the first steps towards the modern welfare state.

THE CRIPPEN CASE

The trial of Dr Harvey Hawley Crippen for the murder of his wife in 1910 gained an unusually high degree of publicity because of the unique manner of his arrest. When police inquiries became too close, Crippen fled to Canada by ship, taking with him his girlfriend, Ethel Le Neve, who was disguised as a boy. Aboard the ship the captain realized Le Neve was a girl, guessed who the couple were and radioed London. A Scotland Yard detective crossed the Atlantic in a faster ship, and Crippen was arrested before his ship reached Canada. This was the first time radio had been used to help catch a criminal. Crippen was brought back to England, tried and hanged for murder, but Le Neve was acquitted of a charge of helping him.

COMMONS AGAINST LORDS

The 1909 budget introduced a supertax on very high incomes and a tax on land ownership. These taxes were to raise money for old age pensions and for building new battleships called dreadnoughts which were needed to match the rising military might of Germany.

This started a severe battle between the Commons and the House of Lords, who rejected the budget. A bill aimed at depriving the Lords of the power of rejecting finance bills was resisted by Conservative peers. Edward VII had worked to reach a compromise, but died leaving the constitutional crisis to be solved. George V, however, finally agreed to create enough new Liberal peers to ensure the Bill would get through. In 1911, the Lords gave way and the budget was passed.

THE TITANIC DISASTER

The *Titanic* set out from Britain on her maiden, or first, voyage to New York City, on April 12, 1912. It was the biggest ship in the world, measuring 269 metres long, with a gross tonnage of 46,328. The liner was described as "unsinkable" because she had a double-bottomed hull with 16 watertight compartments and could still float with any four flooded.

On the night of April 14-15, about 2,570 kilometres northeast of its destination, the liner hit an iceberg, which ripped open her hull. The *Titanic* sank two and a half hours later, with the loss of 1,513 lives. The other 711 people on board were picked up by the liner *Carpathia,* which arrived on the scene 20 minutes later. As a result, safety rules for ships were tightened: every ship must now carry enough lifeboats for everyone on board, whereas the *Titanic* had spaces for less than half its passengers; and ships must maintain a 24-hour radio watch.

Below: **The British luxury liner *Titanic* sank in 1912. A collision with an iceberg caused a 90-metre gash in its hull which led to flooding and eventual sinking. In 1985 the wreckage of the *Titanic* was found 800 kilometres southwest of Newfoundland and photographed.**

The liner was described as "unsinkable" because she had a double-bottomed hull with 16 watertight compartments and could still float with any four flooded.

On the night of April 14-15, about 2,570 kilometres northeast of its destination, the liner hit an iceberg, which ripped open her hull. The *Titanic* sank two and a half hours later, with the loss of 1,513 lives. The other 711 people on board were picked up by the liner *Carpathia,* which arrived on the scene 20 minutes later. As a result, safety rules for ships were tightened: every ship must now carry enough lifeboats for everyone on board, whereas the *Titanic* had spaces for less than half its passengers; and ships must maintain a 24-hour radio watch.

THE SHADOW OF WAR

Ever since the 1880s, there had been growing rivalry between the Germans and the British for territories in Africa. By the end of the century Germany was openly challenging Britain's once vastly superior navy and the British resented this. Both countries competed with each other in building bigger and better battleships. The Russians were also alarmed at Germany's growing

FOCUS ON THE FIRST BRITISH MOVIES

The Lumiere brothers in France gave the first ever film show to a paying audience: in Paris over 100 years ago in 1895. But this was just the beginning. The invention of the movie camera and the development of the technique of story-telling on film was greatly helped by British pioneers. William Dickson, a Scottish assistant working for the American inventor Thomas Edison, produced the first reliable movie camera in 1891. Edison hoped it would be as successful as his phonogram (early record player) and light bulb.

Two Englishmen from Brighton started to move the camera to follow the action (previously cameras were static) and used the first close-up in cinema history – in *Grandma's Reading Glass* (1900).

In *Fire!* (1902) James Williamson, an early film-maker, was the first to combine outdoor location shots with indoor studio scenes.

Above: The *Dreadnought* was completed in 1906 in response to the growing fear of German military shipbuilding. At 20,000 tonnes, with a speed of 22 knots and ten mounted guns, this class of battleship helped Britain's Royal Navy to dominate the world's navies for 40 years.

- **1911** Ramsay MacDonald becomes leader of the Labour Party. Parliament Bill passed; Lords give way. Salaries for MPs. South Wales miners end ten month strike. Railwaymen strike. Shops Act: employees to have half a day off every week in addition to Sunday. First Official Secrets Act. William Morris (later Lord Nuffield) makes first Morris car. August 9th: 100°F in London. First women members of the Royal College of Surgeons. National Insurance Act gives help to those on low incomes

- **1912** Miners and London dockers strike. Commons reject votes for women; protests increase. National Health Insurance introduced. Scott dies reaching South Pole. *Titanic* sinks on maiden voyage, more than 1,500 passengers drown. First London-to-Paris flight. First London underground crash, with 22 injured

RULERS OF BRITAIN

HOUSE	NAME	REIGN	MARRIED	CHILDREN
SAXE-COBURG	Victoria	1837 – 1901	Albert of Saxe-Coburg	Victoria, Edward VII, Alice, Alfred, Helena, Louise, Arthur, Leopold, Beatrice
	Edward VII	1901 – 1910	Alexandra of Denmark	Albert, George V, Louise, Victoria, Maud
	George V	1910 – 1936	Victoria Mary of Teck	Edward VIII, George VI, Mary, Henry, George, John
	The House of Saxe-Coburg became the House of Windsor from 1917			

GLOSSARY

Act a law formally recorded in writing, resulting from a decision taken by a legislative body (such as Parliament)

Boer Dutch South African, or descendant of

cabinet a small group of close advisers to the Crown, eventually becoming a group who formed the policy of government

colony settlement by people in a new territory who are still subject to their country of origin

Commonwealth association of independent nations. Generally refers to those who are or who have been ruled by Britain

Conservative Party in British politics the party evolved from the old Tory party of the 19th century. Opposed to socialism

dominions official title of British self-governing colonies

East India Company trading company given monopoly of eastern trade by Elizabeth I in 1600. Controlled India until British government took over direct authority in 1858

federation states united under a central government for defence, but independent in internal affairs

Industrial Revolution the changes that happened to industry in the 1700s and 1800s as a result of powered machinery and the coming of factories

Labour Party in British politics evolved from the Independent Labour Party formed by Keir Hardie in 1893. Largely supported by trade unions, it was to adopt Socialist ideas during World War I, but remained committed to democracy

Liberal Party one of two major political parties in Britain until the rise of the Labour Party, it was descended from the old Whig party of the 18th and 19th centuries. The Liberals grew fewer in number as the Victorian period progressed

mutiny rebellion or uprising by soldiers or sailors against their superiors

Non-Conformists people who do not agree with the established Church of England (including Catholics). Also called dissenters

Parliament highest body in Britain responsible for making laws, consisting of the House of Lords, House of Commons, and the sovereign

Privy Council a group of people appointed for life by the sovereign to be the Crown's private advisers or councillors.

Protestantism religion of any branch of the Western Church separated from the Roman Catholic Church

sanitation clearing up and cleaning of slums by installing drains, sewers and running water to prevent disease such as cholera; social reformers and government-backed reforms began to improve living conditions in the 1850s.

slums housing built near factories during the Industrial Revolution with no running water or sewage system and families crammed in one or two rooms; disease and death being common

socialism a political theory that favours ownership of all resources – land, industry, property, services, energy etc – by all the people, rather than by private individuals

statute a law or rule made by a body or institution, meant to be permanent and expressed in a formal document; especially an Act of Parliament

suffragettes supporters of votes for women, given particularly to British women who campaigned in the early 1900s for the right to vote

trade unions an association of workers formed to protect their rights and maintain their earnings; started in the 1800s with the Industrial Revolution

viceroy governor of a country or a province who rules in the name of his sovereign or government

Welfare State one in which the government take on full responsibility for its citizens' social welfare – their health, schooling, employment, housing, retirement and so on. In 1906 the Liberal Party introduced free school meals and health visits, old age pensions, better pay and working conditions for poorer people and Labour Exchanges to help the unemployed find work

INDEX

ACKNOWLEDGMENTS

The publisher would like to thank the following for supplying additional illustrations for this book:

Picture research: Alex Goldberg, Elaine Willis

page 6, Guys Hospital, Mary Evans Picture Library;
p12 Charles Dickens, Popperfoto; p13, trade union card, National Museum of Labour History; p17, Berlin Conference, Mary Evans Picture Library;